THE PAINTINGS OF
EUGÈNE DELACROIX
II

THE PAINTINGS OF
EUGÈNE DELACROIX

A Critical Catalogue

1816–1831

Volume II · Plates

LEE JOHNSON

OXFORD · AT THE CLARENDON PRESS

1981

Oxford University Press, Walton Street, Oxford OX2 6DP

OXFORD LONDON GLASGOW
NEW YORK TORONTO MELBOURNE WELLINGTON
KUALA LUMPUR SINGAPORE HONG KONG TOKYO
DELHI BOMBAY CALCUTTA MADRAS KARACHI
NAIROBI DAR ES SALAAM CAPE TOWN

Published in the United States by
Oxford University Press, New York

British Library Cataloguing in Publication Data

Johnson, Lee
The paintings of Eugène Delacroix
Vols. 1 and 2
1. Delacroix, Eugène
I. Title   II. Delacroix, Eugène
759.4   ND553.D33   80-40988
ISBN 0-19-817314-8

Printed in Great Britain
at the University Press, Oxford
by Eric Buckley
Printer to the University

List of Monochrome Plates

Dimensions where given are in cm.

LOST WORKS

DOUBTFUL WORKS

Sources of Photographs

This list includes figures and colour plates which appear in Volume I.

Archives photographiques, pls. 5 (bottom), 12, 52, 56, 77, 104, 125, 130, 136, 145 (top), 165 (top), 178 (bottom), 194, 199; Art Institute of Chicago, pl. 100; Bibliothèque nationale, figs. 12, 23, pls. 46 (top), 65 (top), 133, 145 (bottom), 149 (bottom right), 150 (bottom), 151 (top and bottom), 152, 173 (left), 196, 200 (top); Cleveland Museum of Art, pls. 75, 184; A. Dingjan, The Hague, pl. 94; George Eastman House, pl. 107 (bottom); Syndics of the Fitzwilliam Museum, Cambridge, pls. 1, 7 (bottom), 162; Galerie Bernheim-Jeune, pl. 134 (bottom left); Galerie Daber, pls. 31, 166 (bottom), 181 (bottom); Giraudon, figs. 14, 21, pls. 19, 51, 70, 84, 87, 89, 108, 109, 187; Glasgow Art Gallery and Museum, pl. 179 (bottom); Joslyn Art Museum, pl. 164; Kunsthaus, Zurich, pl. 34; Dr. Peter Nathan, pls. 6, 16, 179 (top); Trustees, The National Gallery, London, pls. 64, 72; National Gallery, Ottawa, fig. 7; National Gallery, Prague, pl. 47; Öffentliche Kunstsammlung, Basle, pl. 49 (bottom); Philadelphia Museum of Art, pls. 66, 68, 76, 78, 131, 163 (top); Photorama, Le Havre, pl. 192; Dr. R. W. Ratcliffe, pls. 85 (top left and right), 134 (bottom right); Reinhart Collection, pls. 101, 186; Réunion des Musées nationaux, Paris, figs. 20, 24, 25, 27, 29, pls. II, III, 2, 3, 22, 33, 116, 117, 126, 127, 128, 135, 151 (top), 165 (bottom), 169 (top); Rijksmuseum Kröller-Müller, pl. 21 (top); San Francisco Museum of Art, pl. 49 (top); Robert Schmit, pls. 32, 173 (right); Smith College Museum of Art, pl. 195; The Tate Gallery, London, pl. 36; Vizzavona, pl. 118; Trustees of the Wallace Collection, London, frontispiece, pls. 98, 102; Walters Art Gallery, Baltimore, pl. 122; Messrs. Wildenstein, pls. 55, 74, 167 (top).

Key to Plate Numbers

Catalogue	Plate	Catalogue	Plate	Catalogue	Plate	Catalogue	Plate
1	1	43	39	84	74	124	108
2	1	44	38	85	74	125	109
3	2	45	37	86	75	(detail) 125	108
4	4	46	37	87	78	126	110
5	3	47	40	88	76	127	111
6	5	48	41	89	77	128	112
7	5	49	42	90	79	129	113
8	6	50	43	91	80	130	114
9	7	51	44	92	81	131	115
10	7	52	45	93	79	132	115
11	8	53	46	94	82	133	116
12	9	54	46	95	83	134	118
13	10	55	47	96	82	135	117
14	11	56	48	97	83	136	118
15	12	57	49	98	84	137	119
16	13	58	49	(detail) 98	85	138	120
17	15	59	50	99	86	139	121
18	16	(detail) 59	51	100	87	140	122
19	17	60	52	101	88	141	123
20	14	61	53	102	90	142	124
21	18	61a	54	(detail) 102	85	143	125
22	19	62	55	103	91	144	126
23	21	63	56	104	94	(detail) 144	127
23a	21	64	58	105	89	145	128
24	20	65	57	106	92	146	129
25	20	66	59	107	93	147	130
26	22	67	60	108	93	148	131
27	23	68	61	109	95	149	132
28	27	69	62	110	96	150	133
29	26	70	63	(detail) 110	85	151	134
30	24	71	64	111	97	152	134
31	25	72	65	112	98	153	135
32	27	73	65	113	99	(detail) 153	134
33	28	74	65	114	100	154	136
34	29	75	66	115	101	155	137
35	30	76	67	116	102	156	137
36	31	77	68	117	103	157	138
37	32	78	69	118	104	158	139
38	33	79	70	119	105	159	140
39	34	80	71	120	106	160	141
40	35	81	71	121	107	161	142
41	36	82	72	122	107	162	143
42	36	83	73	123	107		

LOST WORKS

Catalogue	Plate	Catalogue	Plate	Catalogue	Plate	Catalogue	Plate
L1	144	L46	146	L81	149	L104	153
L3	144	L57	147	L83	149	L107	154
L6	144	L61	147	L86	150	L108	154
L22	145	L63	147	L91	150	L109	155
L34/37	145	L73	148	L92	151	L112	155
L38	146	L75	148	L97	151		
L39	146	L78	148	L98	152		
L45	146	L79	149	L101	153		

DOUBTFUL WORKS

Catalogue	Plate	Catalogue	Plate	Catalogue	Plate	Catalogue	Plate
O1	156	D2	163	D19	197	R29	178
O2	158	D3	165	D20	200	R30	179
O3	159	D4	164	D21	200	R31	179
O4	169	D5	165	R1	160	R32	183
O5	169	D6	170	R2	161	R33	184
O6	175	D7	171	R3	161	R34	185
O7	175	D8	173	R5	163	R35	186
O8	181	D9	172	R10	168	R36	188
O9	189	D10	173	R14	168	R37	187
O10	190	D11	177	R16	166	R39	192
M1	157	D13	182	R17	166	R40	193
M2	160	D14	181	R21	167	R41	194
M3	176	D15	188	R22	167	R42	195
M4	176	D16	191	R25	174	R43	198
M5	180	D17	191	R26	177	R44	199
D1	162	D18	196	R28	178		

PLATE I

Academy Figures, Nudes

Male Academy Figure: Half-length, side view. 40 × 34. (1)

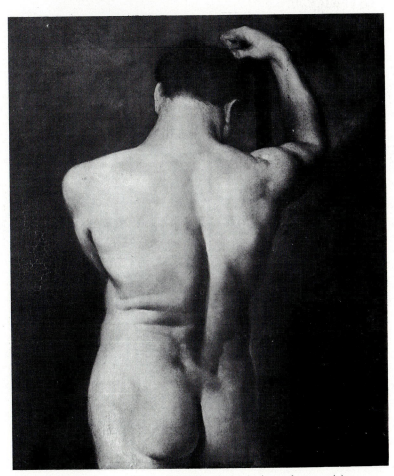

Male Academy Figure: Half-length, back view. 46 × 37.5. (2)

PLATE 2   ACADEMY FIGURES, NUDES

Academy Figure: 'A Blind Man'. 89 × 56.7. (3)

Male Academy Figure, probably Polonais: Standing. 81 × 54. (5)

PLATE 4   ACADEMY FIGURES, NUDES

Female Academy Figure, probably Mlle Rose: Seated, front view. 81·3 × 65·1. (4)

Study of a reclining Female Nude: Back view. 32 × 48. (6)

Female Nude reclining on a Divan ('La Femme aux bas blancs'). 25.9 × 33.2. (7)

PLATE 6   ACADEMY FIGURES, NUDES

A Lady and her Valet. 24.5 × 32.5. (8)

Woman with Parrot. 24.5 × 32.5. (9)

Odalisque reclining on a Divan. 37.8 × 46.4. (10)

PLATE 8

Copies after the Masters

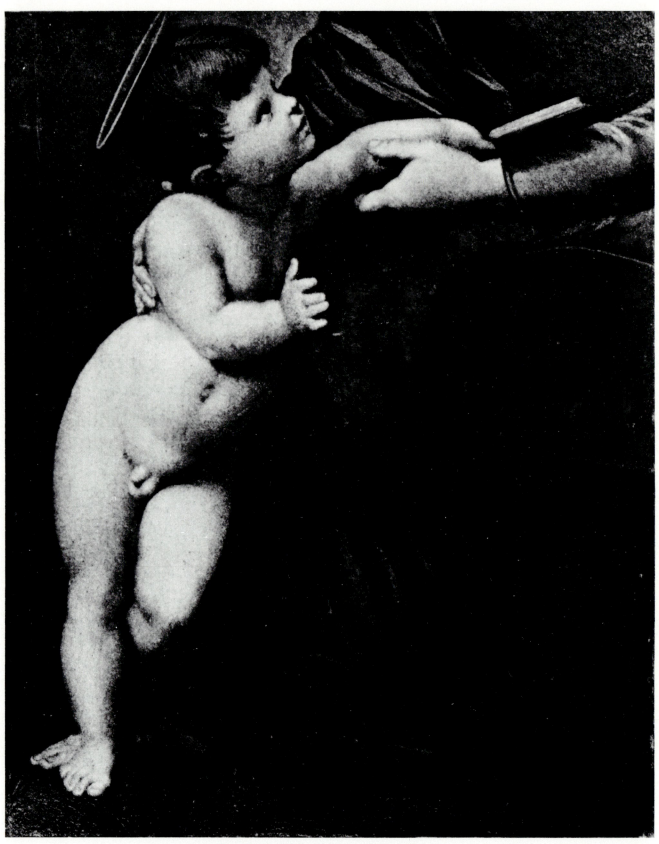

The Christ Child, after Raphael. 60 × 50. (11)

The Entombment, after Titian. 40 × 55.5. (12)

PLATE 10

COPIES AFTER THE MASTERS

Portrait of a Man, after Cariani. 43 × 37. (13)

Two Bearded Heads, after Veronese. 64 × 82. (14)

PLATE 12   COPIES AFTER THE MASTERS

Job tormented by Demons, after Rubens. 62 × 52. (15)

Nereid, after Rubens. 46.5 × 38. (16)

PLATE 14

COPIES AFTER THE MASTERS

Henri IV entrusts the Regency to Maria de' Medici, after Rubens. 89.5 × 116.5. (20)

Conclusion of the Peace, after Rubens. 32.4 × 24.4. (17)

PLATE 16

Satyr embracing a Nymph, after Rubens. 16.5 × 22. (18)

Suzanne Fourment, after Rubens. 65 × 54. (19)

PLATE 18

COPIES AFTER THE MASTERS

Charles II of Spain, after Carreño de Miranda. 116.2 × 89.4. (21)

St. Catherine, after Zurbarán. 81.5 × 65. (22)

PLATE 20

Costume, Accessories, Arms and Armour

Two Studies of an Indian, standing. 36.8 × 45.7. (24)

Two Studies of an Indian, standing and seated. 37.5 × 45.7. (25)

A seated Indian. 36.5 × 27. (23)

A seated Indian. 46.2 × 37.6. (23a)

PLATE 22   COSTUME, ACCESSORIES, ARMS AND ARMOUR

Studies of a Pair of Babouches. 16.6 × 20.6. (26)

Studies of a Turkish Flintlock Gun and Yatagan. 33.5 × 51. (27)

PLATE 24   COSTUME, ACCESSORIES, ARMS AND ARMOUR

Two Studies of a Figure in Greek Costume: Front and side views. 35.2 × 46.4. (30)

Two Studies of a Figure in Greek Costume: Front views. 42.9 × 45.5. (31)

PLATE 26   COSTUME, ACCESSORIES, ARMS AND ARMOUR

Study of a Figure in Greek Costume: Back view. 41 × 31. (29)

Study of a Figure in Greek Costume. 39 × 26.5. (28)

Study of Vicentini in Armour. 24 × 18.5. (32)

PLATE 28

Miscellaneous Orientalia

Seated Figure in Turkish Costume (J. B. Pierret ?). 32 × 24.2. (33)

Turk seated by a Saddle ('Le Turc à la selle'). 41 × 32.8. (34)

PLATE 30

MISCELLANEOUS ORIENTALIA

Turk seated on a Sopha smoking. 24.7 × 30.1 (35)

Turk in a Red Cape. 35.5 × 25.5. (36)

PLATE 32

MISCELLANEOUS ORIENTALIA

Indian Warrior with tethered Horse. 37 × 47. (37)

Young Turk stroking his Horse. 32.7 × 40.7. (38)

PLATE 34

MISCELLANEOUS ORIENTALIA

Indian armed with a Kukri. 40.7 × 32. (39)

Turkish Horseman galloping. 14 × 33. (40)

PLATE 36

Horses and other Animals

Horse standing in a Meadow, facing left. 16.1 × 22.6. (41)

Study of a Horse, facing left. 13 × 19. (42)

A Team of Four Horses. 24.3 × 32.5. (45)

Two Draught-Horses. 28.5 × 39.3. (46)

PLATE 38   HORSES AND OTHER ANIMALS

Study of a Golden Chestnut Stallion. 33 × 25. (44)

Study of a Chestnut Stallion. 33 × 25. (43)

PLATE 40   HORSES AND OTHER ANIMALS

Study of a Brown–Black Horse tethered to a Wall. 52 × 71.9. (47)

Three Studies of a Horse. 45.7 × 37.5. (48)

PLATE 42   HORSES AND OTHER ANIMALS

A Brown Horse, facing left. 46 × 55.7. (49)

Study of a Chestnut and a Grey Horse in a Stable. 32 × 41. (50)

PLATE 44   HORSES AND OTHER ANIMALS

Study of Two Brown and Black Horses in a Stable. 26 × 34.3. (51)

Study of Two Horses. 31.5 × 49.5. (52)

PLATE 46   HORSES AND OTHER ANIMALS

Two Horses fighting in a Meadow. 27 × 32. (53)

Two Horses fighting in the Open. 36.7 × 45.5. (54)

Lion and Tiger. 23.9 × 32.1. (55)

PLATE 48

HORSES AND OTHER ANIMALS

Studies of Lions. 60.7 × 49.8. (56)

Study of a Lioness. 25.1 × 37.8. (57)

Study of a Dead Dog. 41.5 × 87.5. (58)

PLATE 50   HORSES AND OTHER ANIMALS

A Young Tiger playing with its Mother. 131 × 194.5. (59)

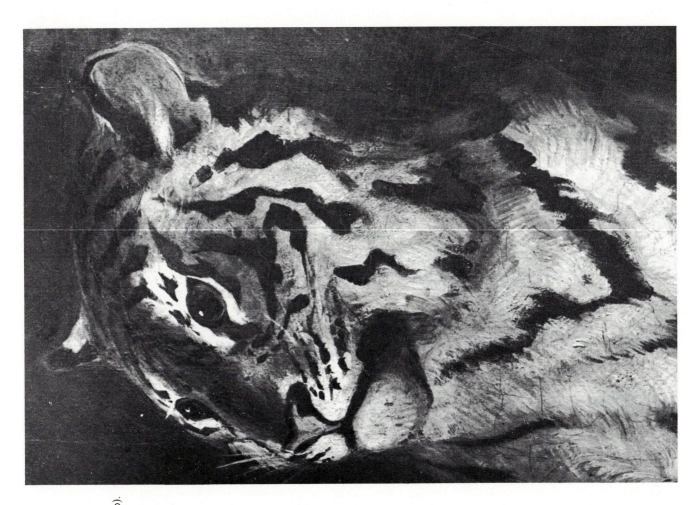

Detail of 59 (plate 50).

PLATE 52

Portraits and Studies of Heads

Head of Actaeon. 25.1 × 21. (60)

Elisabeth Salter. 24.4 × 19. (61)

PLATE 54

PORTRAITS AND STUDIES OF HEADS

Fougerat. 32.3 × 24.3. (61a)

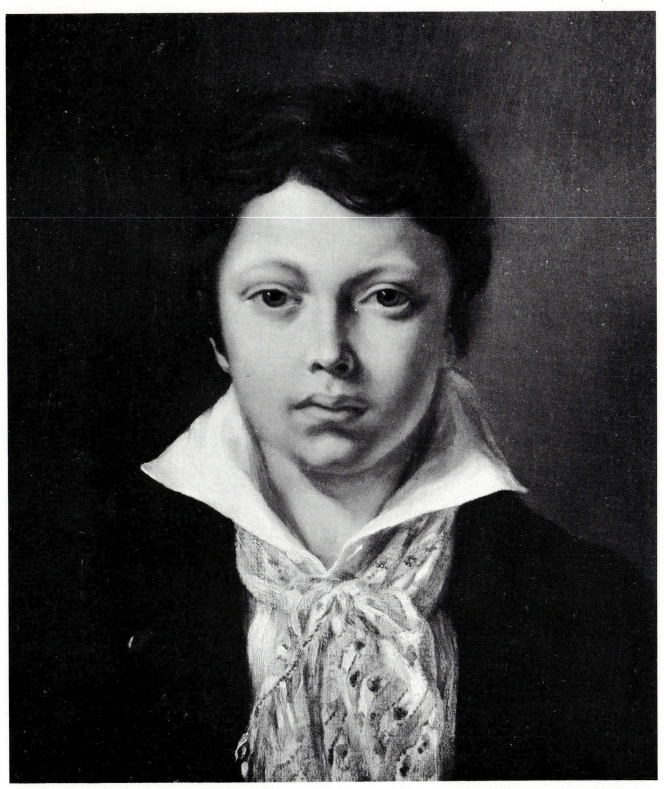

Charles de Verninac. 45.8 × 38. (62)

PLATE 56

PORTRAITS AND STUDIES OF HEADS

Head of a Woman. 44 × 32.6. (63)

Madame Bornot. 65 × 53.7. (65)

PLATE 58

PORTRAITS AND STUDIES OF HEADS

Self-Portrait as Ravenswood. 40.9 × 32.3. (64)

General Charles Delacroix. 39 × 29. (66)

PLATE 60

PORTRAITS AND STUDIES OF HEADS

Jean Baptiste Pierret. 26 × 20. (67)

Henri de Verninac. 59 × 48.8. (68)

PLATE 62

PORTRAITS AND STUDIES OF HEADS

Portrait of a Young Man (Newton Fielding ?). 40 × 32. (69)

Thales Fielding. 32.1 × 24.5. (70)

PLATE 64

PORTRAITS AND STUDIES OF HEADS

Abel Widmer. 59.7 × 48.3. (71)

Auguste Richard de la Hautière.
60 × 50. (73)

Désiré Pellerin. Engraving by
Robaut after Delacroix, 2.8 × 2.3. (72)

Achille Schmitz. Engraving by Robaut after
Delacroix, 2.8 × 2.3. (74)

PLATE 66   PORTRAITS AND STUDIES OF HEADS

Eugène Berny d'Ouville. 61.6 × 50.5. (75)

Amédée Berny d'Ouville. 61.6 × 50.2. (76)

PLATE 68

PORTRAITS AND STUDIES OF HEADS

Head of a Woman (study for the *Massacres of Chios*). 39.4 × 31.8. (77)

Girl seated in a Cemetery. 65.5 × 54.3. (78)

PLATE 70   PORTRAITS AND STUDIES OF HEADS

Aspasie. 81 × 65. (79)

Aspasie. 27 × 21.5. (80)

Aspasie. 32.4 × 24.5. (81)

PLATE 72

PORTRAITS AND STUDIES OF HEADS

Louis Auguste Schwiter. 218 × 143.5. (82)

Charles de Verninac (presumed). 61.5 × 50.5. (83)

PLATE 74

PORTRAITS AND STUDIES OF HEADS

Jenny Le Guillou's Daughter. 46 × 38.2. (84)

Anne Claire Pierret. 41 × 32.4. (85)

Marguerite Juliette Pierret. 39 × 32. (86)

PLATE 76   PORTRAITS AND STUDIES OF HEADS

Woman in a Blue Turban. 59.1 × 48.3. (88)

Young Woman in a Large Hat. 27 × 22. (89)

PLATE 78   PORTRAITS AND STUDIES OF HEADS

Head of an Old Woman (Madame Bornot ?). 39.4 × 32.4. (87)

Head of Dante. 27.4 × 23. (90)

Niccolò Paganini. 45 × 30.4. (93)

PLATE 80   PORTRAITS AND STUDIES OF HEADS

Madame François Simon. 61 × 51. (91)

Charles de Verninac. 61.2 × 50.2. (92)

PLATE 82

Allegory and Decorations

Winter. 44.5 × 84.8. (94)

Summer. 45 × 85. (96)

Autumn. 44.7 × 84.8. (95)

Spring. 44.7 × 84.8. (97)

PLATE 84

Greece on the Ruins of Missolonghi. 209 × 147. (98)

PLATE 85

Don Quixote, detail of 102 (plate 90).

Odette, detail of 110 (plate 96).

Severed Heads, detail of 98 (plate 84).

PLATE 86

Historical and Literary Subjects

The Death of Drusus. (99)

The Barque of Dante, 189 × 246. (100)

PLATE 88   HISTORICAL AND LITERARY SUBJECTS

The Natchez. 90.2 × 117. (101)

Scenes from the Chios Massacres (*Massacres de Scio*). 417 × 354. (105)

PLATE 90   HISTORICAL AND LITERARY SUBJECTS

Don Quixote in his Library. 40 × 32. (102)

The Penance of Jane Shore. 27 × 21. (103)

PLATE 92   HISTORICAL AND LITERARY SUBJECTS

Tasso in the Hosptial of St. Anna. 50 × 61. (106)

Macbeth and the Witches. 33 × 26. (107)

Macbeth and the Witches. 27 × 35. (108)

PLATE 94

HISTORICAL AND LITERARY SUBJECTS

A Battlefield, Evening. 48.3 × 56.5. (104)

Tam o'Shanter. 26.2 × 30.8. (109)

PLATE 96   HISTORICAL AND LITERARY SUBJECTS

Charles VI and Odette. 35.5 × 27.5. (110)

Louis d'Orléans showing his Mistress. 35.2 × 26.8. (111)

PLATE 98

The Execution of Marino Faliero. 146.4 × 114.3. (112)

A Turkish Officer killed in the Mountains. 33 × 41. (113)

PLATE 100

HISTORICAL AND LITERARY SUBJECTS

The Combat of the Giaour and Hassan. 59.6 × 73.4. (114)

Scene from the War between the Turks and Greeks. 65 × 81.5. (115)

PLATE 102   HISTORICAL AND LITERARY SUBJECTS

Mephistopheles appears before Faust. 46 × 38. (116)

The Capulet Ball. 47.2 × 31.1. (117)

PLATE 104   HISTORICAL AND LITERARY SUBJECTS

The Poor Girl. 41 × 37. (118)

Justinian, sketch. 30×21. (119)

Justinian drafting his Laws, sketch. 55 × 45.5. (120)

Robaut after Delacroix, 2.7 × 2.1. (121)

Justinian drafting his Laws, sketch. Anonymous drawing after Delacroix, 11.7 × 9. (122)

Justinian drafting his Laws. Detail from a Photograph, 1855. (123)

PLATE 108   HISTORICAL AND LITERARY SUBJECTS

The Death of Sardanapalus, sketch. 81 × 100. (124)

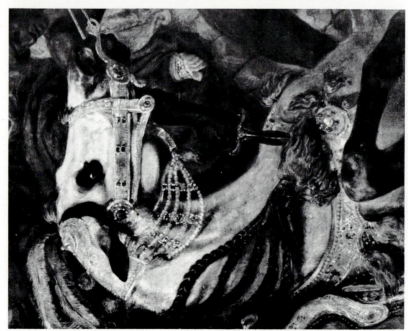

Detail of 125 (plate 109).

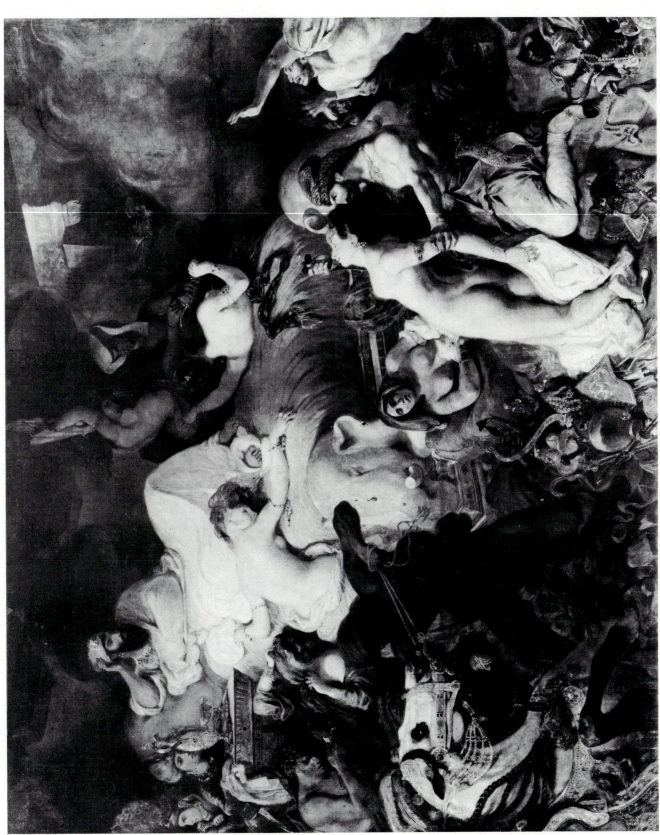

The Death of Sardanapalus. 395 × 495. (125)

PLATE 110   HISTORICAL AND LITERARY SUBJECTS

Henri III at the Death-Bed of Marie de Clèves. 27.5 × 35.5. (126)

Henri IV and Gabrielle d'Estrées. 38.5 × 52.5. (127)

PLATE 112   HISTORICAL AND LITERARY SUBJECTS

Milton dictating 'Paradise Lost'. 80.4 × 64.4. (128)

Cromwell at Windsor Castle. 34.8 × 27.2. (129)

PLATE 114   HISTORICAL AND LITERARY SUBJECTS

Cardinal Richelieu saying Mass, sketch. 37.6 × 27. (130)

Cardinal Richelieu saying Mass. Lithograph by Jourdy after Delacroix,
34.8 × 24.5. (131)

Cardinal Richelieu saying Mass, variant. 40 × 32.4. (132)

PLATE 116   HISTORICAL AND LITERARY SUBJECTS

The Murder of the Bishop of Liège, sketch. 60 × 72.5. (133)

The Murder of the Bishop of Liège. 91 × 116. (135)

PLATE 118   HISTORICAL AND LITERARY SUBJECTS

The Murder of the Bishop of Liège, fragment. 31 × 45.6. (134)

The Murder of the Bishop of Liège, variant. 28 × 39. (136)

Quentin Durward and Le Balafré. 40.5 × 32.4. (137)

PLATE 120   HISTORICAL AND LITERARY SUBJECTS

The Giaour contemplating the Dead Hassan. 22 × 28.2. (138)

Tam o'Shanter. 25.6 × 31.7. (139)

PLATE 122   HISTORICAL AND LITERARY SUBJECTS

The Battle of Poitiers, sketch. 52.8 × 64.8. (140)

PLATE 122   HISTORICAL AND LITERARY SUBJECTS

The Battle of Poitiers. 114 × 146. (141)

PLATE 124   HISTORICAL AND LITERARY SUBJECTS

The Battle of Nancy, sketch. 47 × 68. (142)

The Battle of Nancy. 239 × 359. (143)

PLATE 126   HISTORICAL AND LITERARY SUBJECTS

Liberty leading the People. 260 × 350. (144)

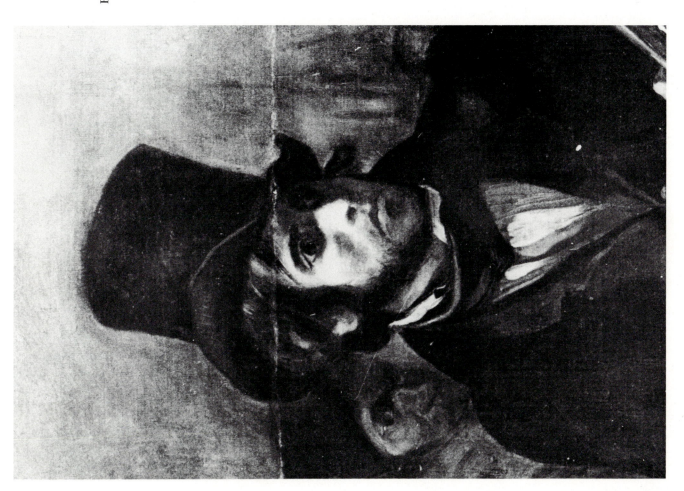

Etienne Arago, detail of 144 (plate 126).

PLATE 128   HISTORICAL AND LITERARY SUBJECTS

Mirabeau and the Marquis de Dreux-Brézé, preliminary sketch. 68.2 × 81.7. (145)

Mirabeau and the Marquis de Dreux-Brézé, final sketch. 77 × 101. (146)

PLATE 130

HISTORICAL AND LITERARY SUBJECTS

Boissy d'Anglas at the National Convention, sketch. 79 × 104. (147)

Interior of a Dominican Convent in Madrid. 130 × 163. (148)

PLATE 132   HISTORICAL AND LITERARY SUBJECTS

Charles V at the Monastery of Yuste. Lithograph by Delacroix after a lost painting, 11.5 × 14.8. (149)

PLATE 133

Religious Paintings

Christ brought before Caiaphas. 28 × 33. (150)

PLATE 134   RELIGIOUS PAINTINGS

The Virgin of the Harvest. 125 × 74. (151)

The Virgin of the Sacred Heart, sketch. 41 × 27. (152)

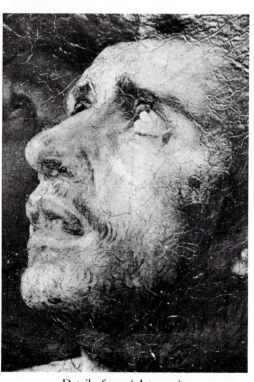

Detail of 153 (plate 135).

The Virgin of the Sacred Heart. 258 × 152. (153)

PLATE 136

The Agony in the Garden. 294 × 362. (154)

Mary Magdalen at the Foot of the Cross. 34 × 26. (155)

Pietà. 24 × 32. (156)

PLATE 138

Ecce Homo. 32 × 24. (157)

PLATE 139

Landscape, Still Life, Genre

The Church of Valmont Abbey. 46 × 38. (158)

PLATE 140   LANDSCAPE, STILL LIFE, GENRE

Landscape with Château, probably Valmont. 17×26.5. (159)

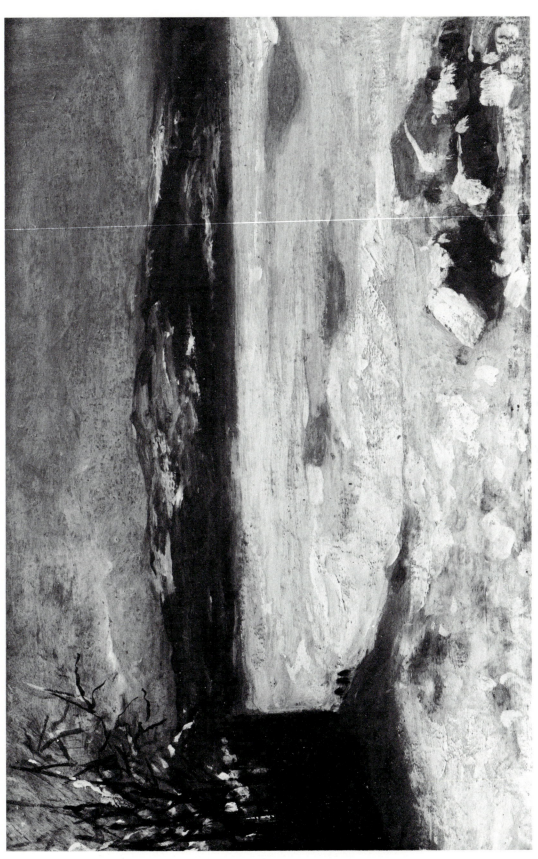

Landscape with Snow. 22.8. × 35.5. (160)

PLATE 142   LANDSCAPE, STILL LIFE, GENRE

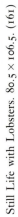

Still Life with Lobsters. 80.5 × 106.5. (161)

A Mortally Wounded Brigand quenches his Thirst. 32.5 × 40.7. (162)

PLATE 144

LOST WORKS

Academy Figures, Nudes

Nude Girl in a Landscape. Lithograph by Robaut after Delacroix, 9.2 × 11.8. (L1). *See page* 175

Woman lying on a Sopha. Drawing by Robaut after Delacroix, 4.4 × 8.4. (L6). *See page* 176

Male Academy Figure. Drawing by Robaut after Delacroix, 15 × 8.3. (L3). *See page* 176

PLATE 145

Copies after the Masters

Jacob and the Flocks of Laban, after the 17th-century Genoese School (?). 61 × 100. (L22). *See page* 181

'Quien mas rendido?', after Goya. Drawing by Robaut after Delacroix, 11 × 14. (L34/37). *See page* 184

PLATE 146

Costume

A Figure in Greek Costume. Engraving by Robaut after
Delacroix, 2.5 × 2. (L38). *See page* 185

Man in Greek Costume in a Landscape. (L39). *See page* 185

Study of a Man in 'Oriental' Costume. Tracing by Robaut
after Delacroix, 33 × 24. (L45). *See page* 186

Study of a Man in 'Oriental' Costume, with Spear. Tracing
by Robaut after Delacroix, 33 × 24. (L46). *See page* 187

PLATE 147

Horses

Study of a Dapple-Grey Horse. Drawing by Robaut after Delacroix, 9.1 × 13.2. (L57). *See page* 189

Study of a Horse's Head. Drawing by Robaut after Delacroix (?), 10.4 × 10.4. (L61). *See page* 191

Studies of Seven Horses. Drawing by Robaut after Delacroix, 15.9 × 19.8. (L63). *See page* 191

PLATE 148

Portraits and Studies of Heads

Charles Soulier. Drawing by Robaut after Delacroix, 29.8 × 20.7. (L73). *See page* 193

Portrait of a Child (Adrien ?). Engraving by Robaut after Delacroix, 2.3 × 1.9. (L75). *See page* 194

Anne Claire Pierret (?). Engraving by Robaut after Delacroix, 2.7 × 2.3. (L78). *See page* 195

Anne Claire Pierret (?). Drawing by Robaut after Delacroix, 10.5 × 9 (frame).
(L79). *See page* 195

Madame Dalton. Engraving by Robaut after Delacroix, 2.6 × 2.2. (L81). *See page* 198

Head of a Young Woman. Drawing by Robaut after
Delacroix, 5 × 4 (frame). (L83). *See page* 199

PLATE 150

Allegory

Nemesis. Engraving by Robaut after Delacroix, 3.2 × 2.5. (L86).
See page 199

Historical and Literary Subjects

Roman Women donating their Jewellery. Drawing by Robaut after Delacroix, 11.3 × 14.5. (L91). *See page* 202

Death of a Roman General (?). Drawing by Robaut after Delacroix, 18.2 × 22.9. (L92). *See page* 202

The Witches' Sabbath, sketch. Tracing by Robaut after Delacroix, 25.5 × 38.5. (L97). *See page* 203

PLATE 152   HISTORICAL AND LITERARY SUBJECTS

Desdemona and Emilia. Tracing by Robaut after Delacroix, 25.2 × 16.7. (L98). *See page* 204

The Finale of *Don Giovanni*. Drawing by Robaut after Delacroix,
20.4 × 17. (L101). *See page* 206

Mazeppa. Engraving by Robaut after Delacroix, 2.7 × 3.5. (L104).
See page 207

PLATE 154

Religious Paintings

Christ before Pilate. Drawing by Robaut after Delacroix, 10 × 15. (L107). *See page* 209

Two Angels. Engraving by Robaut, 2.3 × 3. (L108). *See page* 209

The Agony in the Garden. Drawing by Robaut after Delacroix, 23.3 × 31. (L109). *See page* 210

Jesus and the Paralytic. Drawing by Robaut after
Delacroix, 5.4 × 6.1. (L112). *See page* 210

PLATE 156

DOUBTFUL WORKS
Academy Figures, Nudes or Single Reclining Figures

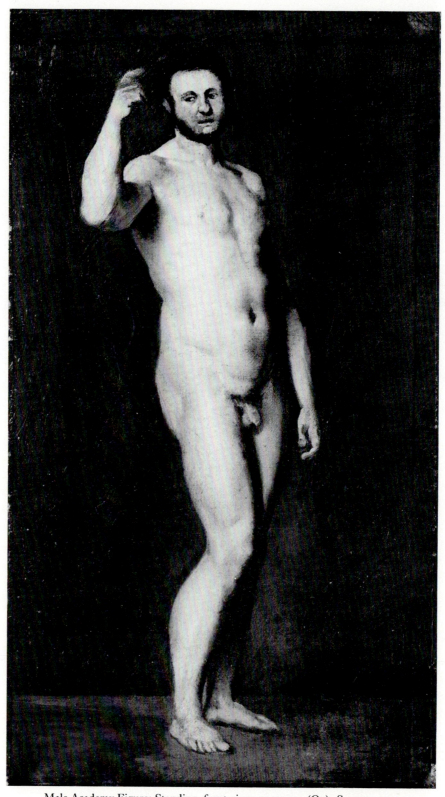

Male Academy Figure: Standing, front view. 55 × 30.3. (O1). *See page* 213

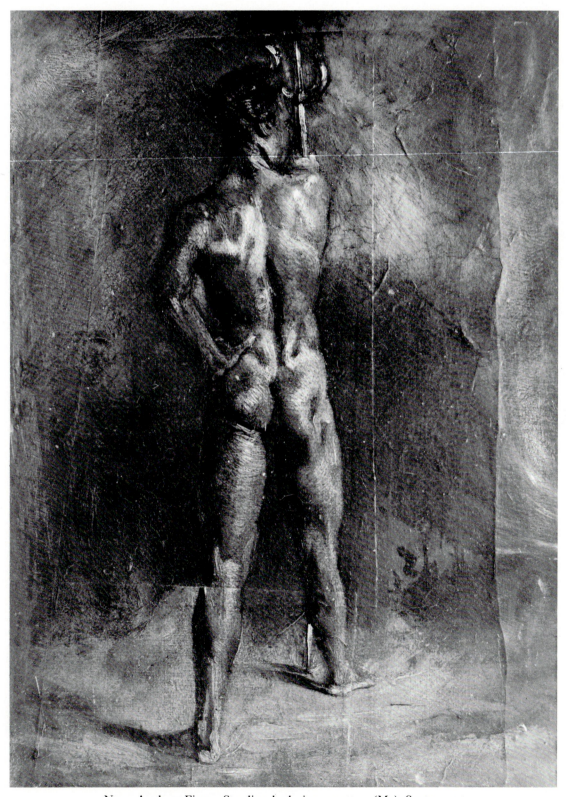

Negro Academy Figure: Standing, back view. 43.5 × 32. (M1). *See page* 215

PLATE 158　　　　　　　ACADEMY FIGURES, NUDES OR SINGLE RECLINING. FIGURES

Female Academy Figure: Seated. 81 × 65. (O2). *See page* 213

Three Life Studies of a Female Nude. 49.2 × 60.5. (O3). *See page* 215

PLATE 160   ACADEMY FIGURES, NUDES OR SINGLE RECLINING FIGURES

Male Academy Figure, probably Polonais: Seated. 81 × 66. (M2). *See page* 216

Male Academy Figure: Standing, front view, hands behind back. 81 × 65. (R1). *See page* 217

Above right. Study of a Woman in Bed. 27.3 × 35. (R2). *See page* 217
Right. Nude Woman reclining on a Divan. 22 × 28.5. (R3). *See page* 218

Study of a Mulatress. 56.5 × 25. (D1). *See page* 216

PLATE 163

Copies after the Masters

Copy after Veronese (*Marriage at Cana*). 64.8 × 81.6. (D2). *See page* 218

Six Studies of Heads, after Veronese (?). 33 × 41. (R5). *See page* 219

PLATE 164

COPIES AFTER THE MASTERS

The Entombment, after Rubens, 71.1 × 53.3. (D4). *See page* 218

Angel, after Rubens. 23.9 × 19. (D3). *See page* 218

Susanna and the Elders, after Rubens. 27 × 35. (D5). *See page* 219

PLATE 166

COPIES AFTER THE MASTERS

Landing of Maria de' Medici at Marseille, after Rubens. 39 × 31. (R17). *See page 222*

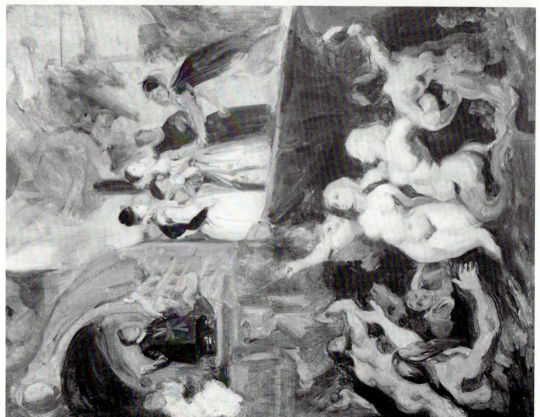

Landing of Maria de' Medici at Marseille, after Rubens. 40 × 32.5. (R16). *See page 222*

Reconciliation of Maria de' Medici and her Son, after Rubens. 29.5 × 22.5. (R22). *See page 223*

Reconciliation of Maria de' Medici and her Son, after Rubens. 61.8 × 51. (R21). *See page 223*

PLATE 168   COPIES AFTER THE MASTERS

A Tourney, after Rubens. 38 × 55. (R14). *See page* 221

Boar Hunt, after Rubens. 54.2 × 71.5. (R10). *See page* 221

PLATE 169

Costume, Accessories, Arms and Armour

A Persian Helmet. 48.7 × 27.2. (O5). *See page* 224

Studies of Armour. 46 × 55. (O4). *See page* 224

PLATE 170

COSTUME, ACCESSORIES, ARMS AND ARMOUR

Study of a Bearded Arab. 24.8 × 20.5. (D6). *See page* 225

Study of a kneeling Figure in Turkish Costume. 43.2 × 32.4. (D7). *See page* 225

PLATE 172   COSTUME, ACCESSORIES, ARMS AND ARMOUR

Two Studies of a Man in Greek Costume. 45.4 × 40. (D9). *See page* 226

A Man in Greek Costume seated by the Sea. 34 × 28. (D8). *See page* 225

Study of a seated Man in Greek Costume. 34.5 × 23.5. (D10). *See page* 226

PLATE 174

Turkish (?) Horseman aiming a Pistol. 30 × 22. (R25). *See page* 227

PLATE 175

Horses

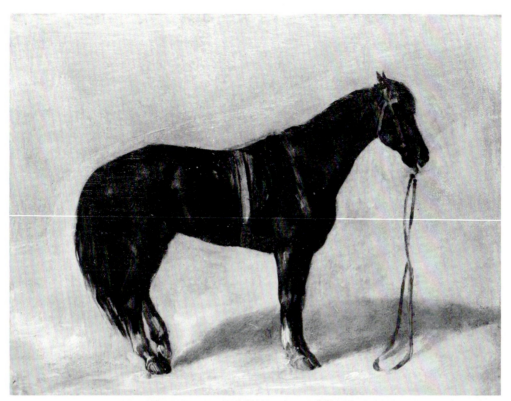

An Arab Horse with Blue Blanket. 19 × 24.5. (O6). *See page* 227

A Roan. 16.5 × 43. (O7). *See page* 227

PLATE 176   HORSES

A Bay attached to a Post in a Field. 19 × 21.3. (M3). *See page* 228

Rump of a Chestnut Horse. 32 × 24.5. (M4). *See page* 228

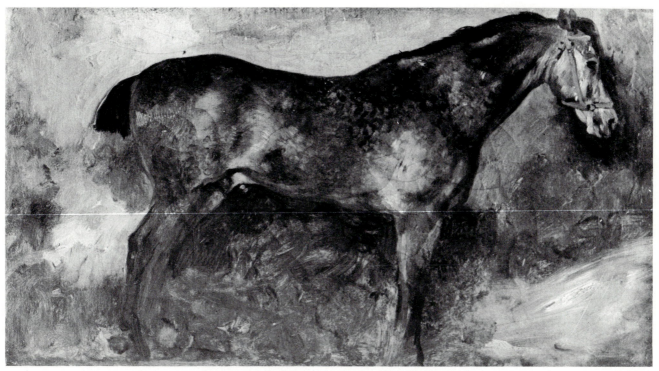

Brown Dappled Horse. 26 × 45. (D11). *See page* 228

A Bay, facing right. 30.5 × 44.5. (R26). *See page* 229

PLATE 178   HORSES

Study of a Horse, facing right. 27 × 21. (R28). *See page* 229

Study of a White Horse. 19.5 × 25. (R29). *See page* 229

Two Horses at a Stable. 24.5 × 19. (R30). *See page* 229

White Horse, probably 'Le Florido'. 45.9 × 55. (R31). *See page* 229

PLATE 180

Portraits and Studies of Heads

Self-Portrait. 35 × 27. (M5). *See page* 231

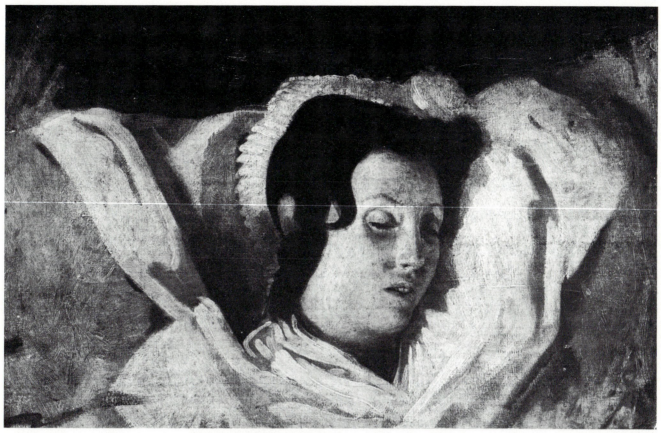

Head of a Woman in Bed. 34.7 × 54. (O8). *See page* 230

Head of a Woman in a Red Turban. 41.3 × 35.2. (D14). *See page* 232

PLATE 182   PORTRAITS AND STUDIES OF HEADS

Portrait of Paul Barroilhet (?) in Turkish Costume. 46.3 × 38. (D13). *See page* 231

Portrait of M. Washington in Greek Costume. 46 × 35. (R32). *See page* 233

PLATE 184

PORTRAITS AND STUDIES OF HEADS

Portrait of Count Demetrius de Palatiano. 41 × 33. (R33). *See page 233*

Portrait of Count Demetrius de Palatiano. 40.2 × 31.6. (R34). *See page* 234

PLATE 186

Allegory

Greece on the Ruins of Missolonghi. 42 × 27.5. (R35). *See page* 235

PLATE 187

Historical and Literary Subjects

Death of Cato. 60 × 44. (R37). *See page* 238

PLATE 188   HISTORICAL AND LITERARY SUBJECTS

The Barque of Dante, sketch. 13.8 × 21. (D15). *See page 237*

The Barque of Dante. 27.3 × 35.5. (R36). *See page 238*

The Witches' Sabbath. 81 × 100. (O9). *See page* 236

PLATE 190   HISTORICAL AND LITERARY SUBJECTS

Combat between Two Horsemen in Armour. 80.7 × 100. (O10). *See page* 236

The Execution of Marino Faliero, sketch. 35 × 27. (D16). *See page 237*

Renaissance Scene. 49 × 75. (D17). *See page 237*

Faust, Wagner and the Poodle. 37.5 × 28.5. (R39). *See page* 239

Faust, Wagner and the Poodle. 41 × 33. (R40). *See page* 239

PLATE 194   HISTORICAL AND LITERARY SUBJECTS

The Murder of the Bishop of Liège, sketch. 60 × 73.5. (R41). *See page 239*

Boissy d'Anglas at the National Convention, sketch. 40·7 × 54·2. (R42). *See page 240*

PLATE 196

Religious Paintings

The Agony in the Garden. 27 × 35. (D18). *See page* 240

PLATE 197

Landscape, Genre, Interiors without Figures

Mountainous Landscape with Tower. 25.3 × 33.3. (D19). *See page* 241

PLATE 198   LANDSCAPE, GENRE, INTERIORS WITHOUT FIGURES

An Attic. 39 × 31. (R43). *See page 242*

Interior with Stove. 51 × 44. (R44). *See page 242*

PLATE 200

LANDSCAPE, GENRE, INTERIORS WITHOUT FIGURES

Interior with Owl. 23 × 31. (D20). *See page* 241

The Poacher. Engraving by Robaut, 3.2 × 2.6. (D21). *See page* 242